NORTH DEVON COAST

IN OLD PHOTOGRAPHS

FROM THE BEAFORD PHOTOGRAPHIC ARCHIVE

NORTH DEVON COAST
IN OLD PHOTOGRAPHS
FROM THE BEAFORD PHOTOGRAPHIC ARCHIVE

COMPILED BY
BERYL YATES

ALAN SUTTON
1989

Alan Sutton Publishing
Gloucester

First published 1989

British Library Cataloguing in Publication Data

North Devon Coast in old photographs.
1. Devon. North Devon, history
I. Beaford Centre
942.3'52

ISBN 0-86299-653-8

Typesetting and origination by
Alan Sutton Publishing.
Printed in Great Britain by
Dotesios Printers Limited.

CONTENTS

William and Elizabeth Liverton (née Griffiths).

This book is dedicated to my great-grandfather, William (Big Bill) Liverton (1836–1912). He was top sawyer and first foreman of Rawle, Gammon & Baker in Barnstaple, starting with them as a young boy when the firm first opened on the Braunton Road. It is through researching him that my love of local history has grown.

INTRODUCTION

In compiling this book, along with its two fellow volumes, I have put myself back into the year 1902, and tried to produce illustrated guide books of that era, with a great deal of help from Kelly's Directory of Devon. I have chosen the year 1902 because the majority of the photographs in our Archive were taken between 1890 and 1910, and so 1902 seemed a reasonably representative middle year. On the general subject of the County of Devon, I extracted the following from Kelly – the briefest of brief histories:

> The earliest inhabitants of Devon are not known, but are supposed to be of Lappish or Finnish origin. At an early period it was occupied by the Iberians, as the names of the rivers – the Tamar, Taw and Tavy – show. Of the early periods there are many relics, as circles of stone, including Grimspound on Dartmoor, and the Scorhill Circle. There are many cromlechs and other monuments of rude stone, and early weapons have been found. The Welsh and the Belgians were gradually overcoming the Iberians, and driving them west, when in the beginning of the Christian era, the Romans made themselves masters of the islands. The tribe they found here was named the Damnoni. The Romans thickly settled the whole of Devon, as the names of places will show. The chief towns were Isca Damnoniorum (now Exeter) and Muridunum.
>
> The chief remains of the roads, known by their English names, are:– Orway, Solway, Oxenway, Farway, Shurway, Broadway, Whiteway, Northway, Elverway, Oldaway, Roadway, Reddaway, Greenway, Ridgway, Helway, Holloway, Harapate or Harepath, Sticklepath, Gappath, Coleridge, Bromridge, Doddridge, Cuttridge, Oldridge, Horridge, Sandridge, Hare-street, Dark-street and Bowstreet. The name of street is not so commonly applied to a Roman road in Devon, as it is in the east of England.
>
> The Roman settlements are so numerous that they would form a long list, about 500 being recognisable. On the downfall of the Romans, the Welsh and mixed Romans were left to themselves, and several West Welsh Kingdoms were formed in Devon and Cornwall, among which war and strife, religious and civil, were constant.
>
> On the English invading Britain, Devon early drew their attention; and in 614, the West Saxons made their first attack. Their progress was slow, and it was not unitl AD 926 that the King of the Cornwelsh was at length driven beyond the Tamar. From 876 to 1003, Devon was, however, wasted by the Danes. At Kenwith Castle, near Northam, are the remains of the old building,

in the attack on which the Danes, under Hubba, were defeated by the Saxons under Alfred, and their standard captured; an old tradition assigns a spot, still known as 'Bloody Corner', as the scene of a duel between two of the chieftains; and at Appledore is the landing-place where the invaders first set foot on this land. Nevertheless, the Welsh in Devon were exterminated, and the old land settled by English. Thus said Kelly.

I had some difficulty in deciding how near or far from the coast villages had to be, to term them coastal; although we have over 7,000 old photographs in our Archive, the majority of them are of inland village locations, and I found I was very low on pictures of some places, e.g. Ilfracombe, and absolutely without reference at all for others such as Combe Martin. I am therefore deeply indebted to Mrs Slocombe, curator of the Ilfracombe Museum, for her kind co-operation and loan of some 60 or 70 photographs of Ilfracombe and the surrounding coastal villages, such as Woolacombe and Mortehoe; I can strongly recommend a visit to The Ilfracombe Museum – to my mind the most fascinating and well-organized small museum I have ever visited, with exhibits ranging from costumes and photographs to brass rubbing (for visitor participation) and many beautiful butterfly collections.

I am afraid some readers will be frustrated and annoyed at the brevity and lack of information contained in some of the photograph captions; this is why I have used Kelly so freely – he gives a very clear concise outline of each village at that time, and one can somehow recapture the tempo of turn-of-the-century life – visitors being met by 'conveyances' at numerous small railway stations, telegraphs being sent, some places being so advanced as to be lit by electricity(!) – and permeating it all, the rigid Victorian conventions of 'gentry', and 'tradesmen' and servants. A very different world!

I am always grateful to receive any information to add to our photographs. I have recently given talks to both the Croyde and Georgeham and the West Down Women's Institutes, and various members have offered to loan us more coastal photographs to copy and add to the Archive, an offer much appreciated.

Finally, I hope people will enjoy looking through these samples of our Archive as much as I have enjoyed compiling the books, and amassing the information.

Beryl Yates

The view towards the New Inn (now renamed), *c.* 1900.

ABBOTSHAM is a parish and village on the southern shore of Barnstaple Bay, 2 miles west from Bideford station on the Torrington branch of the London and South Western railway, in the North Western division of the county, Shebbear hundred, Bideford petty sessional division, union and county court district, rural deanery of Hartland, archdeaconry of Barnstaple and diocese of Exeter. There will be a station on the Bideford, Westward Ho! and Appledore railway about half-mile north-west from the village and near the cliffs. The church of St. Helen is an ancient edifice of stone, in the Early English style, restored and reseated in 1870 and consists of chancel, nave, south porch and an embattled western tower, containing 6 bells; the fifth bears the words "Campana Johannis" in beautifully formed and floriated letters, and the tenor, a very fine-toned bell, has the word "Iemosynary" repeated nine times, reversed or upside down: there are several stained windows: the ends of the benches are finely carved, and exhibit numerous shields with the emblems of "Our Lord's Passion," figures of saints, the Bourchier knot and various initials: there are sittings for 300 persons. The register dates from the year 1653. The living is a vicarage, net yearly value £193, including 38 acres of glebe, with residence, in the gift of and held since 1881 by the Rev. Robert Walpole Sealy M.A. and formerly student of Christ Church, Oxford. The vicarage formed part of the revenues of the monastery of Tavistock, prior to its dissolution in the time of Henry VIII. and was subsequently granted by Queen Elizabeth, in the 6th year of her reign, to the Killigrew family. Here is a Baptist chapel. There are charities of about £14 yearly

The church and village; Miss Bessie Bale is in the trap.

value. Abbotsham cliffs are much resorted to for the advantages of sea bathing in the summer season. Cornborough, the property of Edward Windham Granville Eyre Sealy-Vidal esq. is at present occupied by Major-General John Edward Boyes C.B.; Kenwith is the property and residence of Mrs. Pine-Coffin, of Portledge; near it is a fortification, called Kenwith Castle, besieged by the Danes in the 9th century, but they were defeated, and fled to their ships at Appledore. Abbotsham Court is the property and residence of George John Taylor esq. E. W. G. E. Sealy-Vidal esq. who is lord of the manor, The Misses Turner and Messrs. Charles Colwill Turner, George Turner, William Henry Turner and George John Taylor esqs. and Mrs. Pine-Coffin are the chief landowners. The soil is generally rocky; the subsoil is clay. The chief crops are wheat and oats. The area is 1,878 acres of land and 135 of foreshore; rateable value, £2,542; the population in 1901 was 451.

Sexton, John Cory.

Coombe Walter, half a mile north-west, and Riccards Down, half a mile north, are hamlets.

Buckleigh is also in this parish, for names see Westward Ho!

Post Office.—Mrs. Jane Glover, sub-postmistress. Letters received from Bideford at 7.40 a.m.; dispatched at 6.18 p.m.; sundays, dispatched at 5.18 p.m. Postal orders are issued here, but not paid. The nearest money order & telegraph office is at Bideford, 2 miles distant

National School (mixed), erected in 1851 & since enlarged, for 100 children; average attendance, 60; Charles Hooper, master; Mrs. R. H. Hooper, mistress

Police Station, Frederick Barnacott, constable

PRIVATE RESIDENTS.

Boyes Major-Gen. John Edward C.B. Cornborough
Bromley William Charles, Rixlade
Hall Arthur Hepworth, Old stone
Hibbert Charles R. C. Riccard's dwn
Miles Miss Keen
Pine-Coffin Mrs. (of Portledge), Kenwith
Sealy Rev. Rbt. Walpole M.A.Vicarage
Skinner Miss, Stone house
Taylor George John, Abbotsham court
Turner Charles Colwill, The Barton
Turner Charles Tickle,Coombe Walter
Turner The Misses, Coombe
Vidal Miss, Bowood
Williams Mrs. Coombe cottage

COMMERCIAL.

Backway William Henry, New inn
Bale John, greengrocer & shopkeeper
Barnacott Frederick, police constable
Blight John, farmer, West Pusehill
Brown James, farmer, East Pusehill
Cole John, hind to G. J. Taylor esq. Abbotsham Court farm
Curtis John, farmer, Kenwith farm
Friendship John, shoe maker
Glover Mary Jane & Edith (Misses), milliners & dress makers
Glover Charles, mason
Hearn William, hind to George Turner esq. Rixlade farm
Hooper John, hind to W. H. Turner esq. Greencliff
Heywood George, farmer, Lake
James Edwin, blacksmith
Moase James, farmer & wheelwright
Moore William Heywood, butcher
Pickard Charles Henry, farmer, Bowood farm
Pickard Elizabeth Ann (Miss) & Chas. Henry, jun. farmers, Shamland
Squire William, farmer, Westacott
Taylor Richard, hind to Messrs. C. C. & C. T. Turner, Coombe Walter
Turner Charles Colwill & Charles Tickle, farmers, Coombe Walter
Turner The Misses Mary & Grace, farmers, Coombe
Turner Chas. Colwill,frmr.The Barton
Witheridge Joseph, shoe maker

Pump Lane, *c.* 1900.

The Silver Wedding celebrations of Revd and Mrs Sealy in Butthay Field, 1910. Mrs Church is with Billy in the foreground.

Maypole dancing at the Revd Sealey's silver wedding, 1910.

Rose Cottage 1901. The Barnacott family – they were all policemen!

The Miss Miles and Miss Bay (standing) from Keene, off to a wedding in a donkey trap.

Rixlade Farmhouse, 1915. The marriage of Doris Gregory to Captain Nunning.

Passengers waiting for the train at Kenwith.

The first self-binder at Pusehill.

A school gardening class at Abbotsham in 1912.

Skittles at the Vicarage Fête in 1913.

The Vicarage drawing room.

Keen, c. 1902 (Mr and Mrs Bell are at the window).

Appledore and Bideford Bar – Instow station is in the foreground.

APPLEDORE is a market town and considerable seaport, at the mouth of the rivers Taw and Torridge, 1 mile from Instow station on the Torrington branch of the London and South Western railway, which is on the other side of the river Torridge, over which there is a ferry, and 3 miles north from Bideford, in the North Western division of the county, Shebbear hundred, Bideford petty sessional division and union, Bideford county court district, rural deanery of Hartland, archdeaconry of Barnstaple and diocese of Exeter. The town is lighted with gas by a company and water works are now (1901) in course of construction by the Northam Urban District Council, of which district Appledore forms a ward. Appledore is now a part of the ports of Barnstaple and Bideford, and has two spacious dry docks belonging to the trustees of the late William Yeo, and a patent slip, owned by Robert Cock and Sons, and on the east side of the town, facing Instow, is a broad and spacious quay, which is much frequented; a light railway from Bideford to Westward Ho! and Appledore was begun in 1897. The ecclesiastical parish was formed August 26, 1844, from the civil parish of Northam. The church of St. Mary, erected in 1838, is an edifice of stone in the Early English style, consisting of chancel, nave, north aisle, south porch and a turret containing one bell: there are 364 sittings. The register dates from the year 1844. The living is a vicarage, net yearly value £210, in the gift of the vicar of Northam, and held since 1896 by the Rev. Alfred Gurney Goldsmith M.A. of Trinity Hall, Cambridge. There are Congregational, Baptist and Wesleyan chapels, meeting rooms for the Plymouth Brethren and Bible Christians, a Sailors' rest and a Seamen's mission. The trade principally consists in shipbuilding, and steel and iron barge building, the importation of timber from Norway and Sweden, and limestone from Wales, and the exporting of gravel to South Wales. The Market House was erected in 1848; Wednesday and Saturday are the market days. The early closing day is on Wednesday at 4 p.m. The Public Rooms in West Appledore, erected in 1894, will hold 500 persons. The large collar and cuff factory of Messrs. Vincent and Duncan employs over 100 females. At West Appledore is a battery, constructed in June, 1895, for the use of the Royal Naval Reserve here; near the battery is the boat-house of the Royal National Life Boat Institution, and at Rock Point is the Custom House. Here is also a coastguard station. Salmon and codfish are caught in great quantities, and a number of the inhabitants obtain their livelihood by collecting mussels and cockles, which are found on the sands at Braunton, and also a species of seaweed called "laver," which is much in request. In the neighbourhood is the Hubblestone rock, supposed to have been the burial place of the Danish chief Hubba, who was slain near the coast A.D. 377-8. Richmond House, a handsome modern mansion commanding fine sea and land views, is at present (1901) unoccupied. The trustees of the late William Yeo, Mr. Oliver Heywood and the trustees of the late Sidney Cartwright esq. are the principal landowners. The area is 130 acres; rateable value, with Northam, £15,861; the population in 1891 was 2,440.

Parish Clerk, John Slader.

Post, M. O. & T. O., T. M. O., S. B., Express & Parcel Delivery, Annuity & Insurance Office (Railway Sub-Office. Letters should have R.S.O. North Devon added.)—William John Land, sub-postmaster. Letters arrive from London at 6.0 a.m.; north mail at 11.45 a.m. & 5.20 p.m., dispatched at 9.0 a.m. & 1.10 & 7.15 p.m. Money orders are granted & paid from 7 a.m. to 8 p.m. This post office is in direct telephonic communication with Westward Ho! Peppercombe, Clovelly, Barnstaple, Croyde, Lundy Island & coastguard station

Wall Letter Boxes, West Appledore & Myrtle st. cleared at 8.45 a.m. & 1 & 6.30 p.m.; sundays, 8.45 a.m

PUBLIC ESTABLISHMENTS.

Custom House, Samuel Hernaman Martin R.N.R. supt

Market Hall

Police Station, Bude street, Josiah Evans Sanders, const

Public Rooms, West Appledore, Harold Robert Moody, proprietor

R.N.R. Battery, John Wright R.N. chief officer

PUBLIC OFFICERS.

Admiralty Surgeon & Agent & Medical Officer & Public Vaccinator, Northam District, Bideford Union, Allan Edward Mahood M.B., F.R.C.S.Eng. Northam house, Northam

Chief Officer, Coast Guard, John Wright

Medical Officer of Health to Northam Urban District Council, Allan Edward Mahood M.B. & M.Ch., R.U.I., F.R.C.S.Eng. Northam house, Northam, Bideford

Surveyor to Lloyd's, George Westcott, Odun road

The *Lord Rolle*, Bideford.

Appledore Quay.

Appledore fishergirls.

Bude Street, Appledore.

The Market – the market house was erected in 1848.

There are three pages of Kelly's Directory devoted to Barnstaple; here are some of the more interesting details: 'Barnstaple is a sub-port in North Devon of the Bristol district ... 203¼ miles from London by the Great Western Railway ... the railway stations are just without the town, the Great Western on the east and the South Western on the south; there is also a station for the latter on the quay called the "Town" station. A narrow gauge railway, 19½ miles in length was opened for May 11th 1898, between Barnstaple and Lynton. The town ... on the north bank of the river Taw is well built, with wide and cleanly streets, lighted by gas ... from works in the Barbican, and is supplied by water from a stream rising above Chelfam Bridge, in Shirwell Park ... there are two reservoirs, one at Raleigh Park ... and the other at Pickards Down, Barnstaple.'

The Square. 'The Albert Clock tower, standing in the irregular open space at the entrance to the town from the bridge, called the square, was erected by public subscription in memory of HRH the Prince Consort (date 14th December 1861) and contains a clock with four illuminated dials; at the base is a drinking fountain in coloured marbles, with an inscription

in encaustic letters. The square was enclosed by a handsome ornamental iron railing in 1879 . . . and has been tastefully laid out with walks, and a fountain constructed in the centre.' (Kelly.)

The promenade beside the Taw in Rock Park.

'Barnstaple bridge, generally supposed to have been erected about the 12th or 13th century is a fine structure of 16 arches, and was widened in 1834 . . . it is maintained by the Bridge trustees.'

The limits of the boundary of the port of Barnstaple are defined, and Kelly states that 'The trade of the port is very small, the only import being timber from Norway, Sweden, Canada and U S A . . . . There is also a coasting trade in coal from S. Wales and a little general merchandise from Ireland; the number of vessels cleared at Barnstaple in 1900 was 952, and the tonnage 54,932 . . . there were 21 fishing boats registered; these employed 49 men and boys . . . .'

Rock Park, with Holy Trinity Church in the background.

'The parish church of SS Peter and Paul, standing nearly in the centre of the town is an ancient edifice of stone, in the Gothic style .... Holy Trinity is an ecclesiastical parish formed in 1846. The original church ... completed in 1847, partially collapsed in 1867 owing to a subsidence of the foundations ..., and was rebuilt on a somewhat different plan in 1867. St Mary Magdalene is an ecclesiastical parish, formed in 1844; the church was erected in 1846, in the Early English style ... Newport is also an ecclesiastical parish, formed in 1847, from the civil parish of Bishops Tawton, with its church of St John the Baptist.'

There were also the following churches: the Catholic church, near Trinity Street, built in 1885; the Reformed Episcopal church, in Summerland Street, built in 1880; the Wesleyan chapel, in Boutport Street, built in 1811 and enlarged in 1868; the congregational chapel in Cross Street, founded in 1705 and rebuilt in 1870 'on an enlarged scale in a Continental Gothic style'. There was also a Baptist chapel in Boutport Street, built in 1833; the Brethren's place of worship in Grosvenor Street, 1840, and the Bible Christian chapel in Bear Street, 1876. The cemetery in Bear Street is five acres in extent and contains two mortuary chapels.

'The Penrose Almshouses, in Litchdon Street, founded in 1624 by John Penrose, a merchant of Barnstaple, consist of twenty dwellings for two inmates in each, with a small garden plot attached to each dwelling. There are also in the town, Paige's Almshouse in Church Lane, Horwood's Almshouses in Church Lane, founded in 1674, and Salem Almshouses in Trinity Street, built in 1834.' (Kelly.)

The High Street, *c.* 1910.

Queen Anne's walk.

Looking across the Taw; an early photograph of the Quay, showing Queen Anne's walk and the bottom of Cross Street, *c.* 1870.

The Pannier Market. 'The New Market in High Street comprises a lofty and well-ventilated arcaded hall, almost 320 feet long by 70 feet wide, for vegetables and general produce . . . and attached to the main building are corn and seed markets, with a music hall above, capable of containing 1,000 persons.' (Kelly.)

Butcher's Row. 'Adjoining the main market are 33 butcher's shops, with a covered walk in front, an avenue separating them from the vegetable market. The market is held on Tuesdays and Fridays for vegetables, and Fridays only for corn and cattle.' (Kelly.)

From an etching of the Guildhall. The present Guildhall in High Street was built in 1826, and contained a 'spacious council chamber, jury rooms and a police station and superintendent's office beneath'. (Kelly.)

An artist's impression of Old Barnstaple Fair.

Barum Fair, *c.* 1910. 'The Annual Fair commences on the first Wednesday preceding the 20th September, and continues during three days. The cattle fair is held in the cattle market; the horse fair on the Quay, and the pleasure fair on the North Walk.' (Kelly.)

A steam traction engine in Boutport Street, *c.* 1906. It is reputed to be pulling a Sunday School outing from Lovacott to Instow; the engine was owned by John P. Downing, farmer and proprietor of steam rollers, traction and thrashing machines, and steam sawing machinery, of East Barton, Horwood.

The north end of High Street, *c.* 1900.

The Bath and West of England show was held in Barnstaple in 1859, on the site that is now the Pottington Estate.

The Bath and West Show, 1859. Note the entrance to the Arts Department in the background – the forerunner probably of the Art and Craft Tent at today's shows. Imagine trundling round a County Show today in a crinoline, or top hat and frock coat.

Cross Street and Southgate (now demolished) showing the timber-framed house on the right – note the statue of Queen Anne in the background through the arch.

A drawing of the timber-framed house in Cross Street.

A photograph of the same building being demolished.

M. Squire and Son, of Salem House, were listed in Kelly's 1902 as being 'agricultural and horticultural implement dealers, manure and cake merchants'. This photograph from our archive accompanied a postcard dated 1910, which read: Dear Sir, we shall be sending the 4 tons manure you kindly ordered tomorrow afternoon (Wednesday) per motor. Yours faithfully, M. Squire & Son.

The Barnstaple and district Motor Cycle and Light Car Club, outside the Atheneum in 1920. (Note – a further building on the right of the Atheneum (now the North Devon Museum) is now a small garden area.) Kelly says of the Atheneum: 'The North Devon Atheneum, established in place of the Literary Institute, founded in 1845, now occupies the premises at the Bridge end, purchased and presented by W.F. Rock in 1888, and to be held in trust for ever.'

Boutport Street in September 1938.

War Savings Week – a group in the Square, 1943.

The Cyprus Terrace Infants School, *c.* 1911.

Looking down Newport Road, *c.* 1910.

From a painting of the Rose and Crown at the top of Newport Road.

The Rose and Crown, before the hollow oak was cut down.

Post Office at Bickington.

The Quay Station at Fremington? This is an artist's impression of what I think may have been Fremington Quay, between Instow and Barnstaple.

BISHOP'S TAWTON is a parish and village, on the east bank of the river Taw, 2 miles south-by-east from Barnstaple stations on the London and South Western and Great Western railways, in the North Western division of the county, South Molton hundred, Braunton petty sessional division, Barnstaple union and county court district, rural deanery and archdeaconry of Barnstaple and diocese of Exeter. The church of St. John the Baptist is a building of stone, in the Decorated and Perpendicular styles, consisting of chancel, nave, north aisle, south porch and a tower on the north side with pinnacles and spire, containing a clock and 6 bells, dating from 1803 to 1852: there are memorial windows and various ancient monuments to members of the Chichester family and to the late Rev. John Durand Baker, a former vicar: the church was restored in 1866, and has 350 sittings. The register dates from the year 1558. The living is a vicarage, net yearly value £385, including 26 acres of glebe, with residence, in the gift of the Bishop of Exeter, and held since 1896 by the Rev. Peter Nettleton Leakey M.A. of Corpus Christi college, Cambridge. There is also a church on the Chichester estate, built in 1888 by Charles and Beatrice Chichester: it affords 160 sittings. The charities amount to £13. Hall, the seat of Charles Chichester esq. D.L., J.P. is a fine mansion, beautifully situated on an eminence and commanding a fine view of

the valley of the Taw. It contains a galleried banqueting hall, with rich oak carving dating from 1513, as well as many interesting relics, including a carved oak bedstead, with pillars and tester. The Duke of Bedford, who is lord of the manor, and Charles Chichester esq. are chief landowners. The soil is light; subsoil, gravel and clay. The chief crops are wheat, oats, barley, turnips &c.; there is beautiful grazing land. The area is 3,864 acres of land, 17 of water, 12 of tidal water and 2 of foreshore; assessable value, £3,993; the population in 1901 was 780. Newport, formerly in this parish, was transferred to that of Barnstaple by Local Government Board Order 15,901, March 25, 1885.

Sexton, John Beer.

Post Office.—Mrs. Mary Dunning, sub-postmistress. Letters received from Barnstaple at 7.30 a.m.; dispatched at 6 p.m. Postal orders are issued here, but not paid. Barnstaple is the nearest telegraph office, 3 miles distant, & Newport the nearest money order office

Schools:—

A School Board of 5 members was formed February 14, 1885; Thomas G. Yole, 11 The Strand, clerk to the board

Board (mixed), Herner, built in 1874, for 80 children; average attendance, 31; Miss Gould, mistress

Board (mixed), built in 1841 for 120 children; average attendance, 90; Richd. Taylor, master; Miss Margaret Duffey and Miss Priscilla Robins, mistresses

PRIVATE RESIDENTS.

Baker Mrs. The Cottage
Chichester Charles D.L., J.P. Hall
Davie Major George Christopher F.R.G.S., J.P. The Elms
Foster John Armstrong F.Z.S. Chestwood hill
Holland Richard, Little Pill
Impey Maurice, Westacott cottages
Leakey Rev. Peter Nettleton M.A. Vicarage
Snow George, Little Fisherton
Tamlyn John, Rose Hill villa
Taylor Richard, King's cottage
Western Mrs
Wigram Eustace, Mount Sandford

COMMERCIAL.

Baker William, farmer, Yeo town
Beer Walter, farmer, Pill
Beer John, carpenter
Bond Samuel, farmer, Westacott
Buckingham William, farmer, Shilstone
Challacombe Thomas, farmer, Fisherton
Challacombe Wm. farmer, Hill farm
Darch William Henry, miller (water) corn dealer, Whitemoor mill
Dunn Samuel, farmer, New house
Dunning Mrs. Mary, sub-postmistress
Dyer Jn. jun. frmr.& btchr. Ramally
Dyer John, sen. cattle dealer & farmer
Edgar Ernest, tailor & draper
Featherstone John, carpenter
Gaydon Joseph, farmer, Coddon
Gregory John, market gardener
Hartnoll Nicholas, market gardener
Hookway Albert, farmer, Court farm
Hookway John, farmer, Heaton
Houle John, farmer, Emmetts
Huxtable Anthony, farmer, Downrew
Joslin Francis, frmr. Great Woolstone
Lee John, farmer, Overton farm
Lock George, farmer, Upcott
Manley John, farmer & contractor
Morris Richard, market gardener
Morrish John, builder
Newton Walter, Three Pigeons P.H
Nott Ann (Mrs.), apartmts. New brdg
Odam William, farmer, Broadmoor
Pearce William, builder
Pile Jas. market gardnr. New bridge
Pugsley Francis, carpenter
Bidd Richard, Chichester Arms P.H
Rodd Steven, thatcher
Sanders Robt. Bryant, farmer, Whitemoor farm
Scott John, farmer & timber merchant
Sexton Thos. market gardener & tailor
Smaldon Robert, shopkeeper
Smith John William, farmer, Wellesley barton
Snell John, market gardener
Steer George, farmer & road contractor, Hill
Tatham Fras. Walkingham, frmr. Beara
Thomas Geo. Hy. smith & machinist
Tucker James, farmer, Cross farm
Tucker William, farmer & farm bailiff to Charles Chichester esq. D.L., J.P. Halmston Barton
Vodden George, shoe maker
Wills James, farmer, West Downrew

Kelly's states that 'Bideford – By-the-Ford – is a municipal borough, market town and parish, on the river Torridge . . . 215 miles from London . . . in the hundred of Shebbear and the rural deanery of Hartland.. . . The town is picturesquely seated at the foot of a hill, and is divided into two unequal portions by the river Torridge . . . over which is a noble bridge of 24 arches, 677 feet in length . . . in 1865 it was widened 10 feet by adding footpaths to each side, at an expense of £5,000.. . . A light railway from the quay at Bideford to Abbotsham Cliffs and Westward Ho! was opened in May 1901 . . ..'

Kelly also mentions the Bridge Hall, at the Bridge End, erected in 1882 at a cost of £4,300; the Public Rooms, erected 1871, in Bridgeland Street, comprising a music hall with orchestra; the County Police station in New Road, built in 1897 and containing quarters for a sergeant, one married and four single constables, and cells for three prisoners; the Masonic Hall and the Conservative Club, both in Bridgeland Street; also the Market which was built in 1884, at a cost of £3,000, which houses a Fish Market, a Corn Exchange, a butcher's row and a Pannier Market; also the Cattle Market and the Public Slaughter house which were erected by the Corporation in 1898.

Welcome – the floral arch. This is a particularly interesting photograph as it was taken on 23 May 1907 on the occasion of the Devon County Agricultural Society holding its annual show at the Moreton Estate on the Clovelly Road; the *Journal Herald* of that week stated that 'visitors to the exhibition have to wend their way over the historic bridge . . . at the Town end of which is an arch of massive proportions, the evergreens being relieved with a series of small flags'.

The Bank, Bideford, *c.* 1906.

Bideford Quay, *c.* 1906.

The Quay and Light Railway, early 1900s. The Bideford, Westward Ho! and Appledore Light Railway Company was opened in 1901, extended to Appledore in 1908 and closed in 1916.

Bideford viewed from East-the-Water.

Watching the engine on its way to Westward Ho!, before being taken over to France, presumably in 1914.

Kelly states that Bideford 'is the headquarters of the "D" squadron, Royal North Devon Yeomanry (Hussars) and of the "E" and "H" Companies, 4th Volunteer Battalion Devonshire Regiment; the latter have a drill hall in Torridge Hill'.

Port of Bideford; the tug *Admiral* of Liverpool is in the foreground.

The Quay, Bideford, *c.* 1930.

Proclamation from the balcony of the New Inn; event unknown.

High Street, Bideford.

Looking up the High Street, 1907.

High Street, Bideford, *c.* 1930.

Bideford Town Silver Band Jubilee, 6 May 1935 – 7a.m.!

Torrington Band – Meddon Street opposite the Centric Shop. Left to right: Joe Jenkins, Pasha Baker, Tom Piper, John Gilbert, J. Isaac, Jack Parkhouse, Charlie Noman, Bill Reed, Mr Penney.

Butterworth Minstrels.

A cottage door in Honestone Street.

The Old Ship Tavern, latterly the Rose of Torridge Restaurant, renowned for its old world charm and hospitality, and now transformed into a fast food take-away and fish and chip shop.

Looking down the High Street, the clock was above the Post Office entrance.

The Post Office in 1890.

'The Post Office in High Street was erected in 1886.. . . There is now no shipbuilding here . . . but the prosperity of the town has greatly increased since 1883 by the rapid development of the cuff and collar industry . . . there is also an iron foundry . . . a small pottery, a tannery and a number of malting establishments. There are four banks and a savings bank.. . . The Infirmary and Dispensary in Meddon Street . . . was opened 31st March 1887, in commemoration of the Queen's Jubilee, and was extended in 1895. The Infirmary is available for 22 patients; during the year 1900, 607 out-patients and 339 in-patients were under treatment.' (Kelly.)

The Devon Yeomanry.

The Yeomanry leaving for camp.

The Technical School in 1912; it was later known as Bideford Art School.

The opening of the new post office in 1959.

Elliott's Garage.

Elliott's Garage.

The hill climb.

Pew ends in St Brannocks.

BRAUNTON is a parish and village, on the banks of a rivulet, with a station on the Ilfracombe branch of the South Western railway, 2 miles from the coast and Taw estuary, 5½ north-west from Barnstaple, 8 south from Ilfracombe and 217 from London, and is the head of the petty sessional division, in the North Western division of the county, Braunton hundred, Barnstaple union and county court district and in the rural deanery and archdeaconry of Barnstaple and diocese of Exeter. The church of St. Brannock is a large and ancient building of stone, in the Early English and Perpendicular styles, consisting of chancel and nave and transepts, north and south porches and a tower on the south side with spire, containing a clock and 8 bells: the nave has a panelled oak roof of considerable span, repaired about 1850, and exhibiting on one of its panels a carved representation of a sow with a litter of pigs, alluding to a tradition that St. Brannock, who preached Christianity here A.D. 300, was directed, in a dream, to build a church on the spot where he should first meet such a group: there is an interesting palimpsest brass, having on one side the effigy of a knight in bascinet and camail, c. 1200, and on the other the effigy of a lady kneeling at a prie-dieu; this is inlaid above a stepped cross incised in a large stone

A Braunton village street.

slab, and at the foot is a brass inscription to Lady Elizabeth Bowcer (Bourchier), daughter of John, 1st Earl of Bath, and wife of Edward Chichester esq. ob. 24th August, 1548: the church contains some of the finest examples of wood carving in Devonshire, especially on the bench ends in the nave; a new organ was erected in 1896 by public subscription: in 1887 the nave of the church was new-roofed and the bells rehung, with the addition of two new ones, at an expense of £1,000, under the direction of Mr. William White F.S.A. architect, of London: the south transept, formed by the ground storey of the tower, has also been restored, in memory of Mr. Edward Mock, by his widow, and the chancel by the late Mr. Ewan Christian: a heating apparatus was fixed in 1893, the cost being defrayed by subscription: there are 450 sittings. The register dates from the year 1538. The living is a vicarage, net yearly value £330, including residence, in the gift of the Bishop of Exeter, and held since 1890 by the Rev. Edward Robert Gotto M.A. of Trinity College, Cambridge. On a neighbouring hill are some remains of an ancient chapel, said to have been built by St. Brannock, and known as "St. Anne's chapel." Here are Congregational and Wesleyan chapels and a meeting room for the Brethren. The charities amount to £30 yearly. Near the sea is a large sandy tract of land called "Braunton Burrows," abounding with rabbits: here is also a lighthouse and a lifeboat station. The Earl of Devon, the trustees of the late Lord Rolle (d. 1842) and the Ecclesiastical Commissioners are lords of the manor; and Mrs. Incledon-Webber, Sir William Robert Williams bart. of Upcott House, Barnstaple; Augustus Langham Christie esq. of 42 Great Cumberland place, London W.; Mrs. Basset and J. W. Gifford esq. of Chard, are the chief landowners. The soil is sandy loam; the subsoil is clayey. The chief crops are wheat, barley, potatoes and root crops. The area is 10,265 acres of land, 17 of water, 82 of tidal water and 1,393 of foreshore; rateable value, £12,136; the population in 1891 was 2,171.

The hamlets are:—Bearcharter, 2 miles north-east; Pipacott, 2½ east; Hallsinger, 2 north-east; Winsham, 1½ north-east; Knowle, 1 north; Nethercott, 1½ north-west; Saunton, 2 north-west-by-west and Lobb, 1½ miles north-west.

Saunton Sands, 3 miles north-west-by-west, is an extension of Saunton, and has a small mission church, served by the clergy of Braunton.

Sexton, John Passmore.

Post, M. O. & T. O., T. M. O., S. B., Express & Parcel Delivery & Annuity & Insurance Office (Railway Sub-Office. Letters should have R.S.O. North Devon added). Mrs. Mary Alice Clarke, sub-postmistress. Letters received at 5.50 & 11.45 a.m. & 4.40 p.m.; dispatched at 9.10 a.m. & 1.35 & 7.35 p.m. No post on sunday

Wall Letter Box, Knowle, cleared at 10 a.m. & 6.35 p.m.; no collection on sunday

Post Office, Saunton.—William J. L. Jeffery, sub-postmaster. Letters arrive from Braunton R.S.O. North Devon at 8 a.m. & 5.30 p.m.; dispatched at 12.35 & 6.35 p.m. Postal orders are issued here, but not paid. Braunton is the nearest money order office & Croyde the nearest telegraph office, 2 miles distant

Looking up Chapel Street: the cottages on the left are now ruinous. One of the cottages on the right was a carpenter's shop.

BUCKS MILLS is an ecclesiastical parish, formed April 29, 1862, from the civil parishes of Parkham and Woolfardisworthy, and is on the coast of Bideford bay, 8 miles west from Bideford station on the Torrington branch of the London and South Western railway, in the North Western division of the county, Hartland hundred, Bideford petty sessional division, union and county court district, rural deanery of Hartland, archdeaconry of Barnstaple and diocese of Exeter. The church of St. Anne is an edifice of stone in the Early English style, built and endowed by the late Mrs. Elwes, and consists of chancel, nave, south porch and a tower on the north side of the chancel, containing one bell: the tower was restored in 1887: there are 130 sittings. The register dates from the year 1866. The living is a vicarage, net yearly value £192, including 17 acres of glebe, with residence, in the gift of Richard James Cary-Elwes esq. and held since 1895 by the Rev. David Hughes M.A. of Queens' College, Cambridge. Here is a small Wesleyan chapel. The interest of £1,000, left by Mrs. Elwes, is for medical aid to the poor, afforded under the direction of the vicar; there is also the interest of £100, which is divided between the North Devon Infirmary and Bideford Hospital and the parish Clothing Club. Walland Cary, the seat of Richard James Cary-Elwes esq. J.P. the principal landowner, is a modern mansion situated in beautifully-wooded grounds on the shore of the Bristol Channel. The soil is heavy loam; subsoil, clay and rock. The chief crops are roots and oats. The area is 1,100 acres; the population in 1891 was 250.

Sexton, Dennis Dark.

Post & T. O. & Express Delivery, Bucks Cross.—Wm. Jenn, sub-postmaster. Letters through Bideford, delivered at 8.40 a.m.; dispatched at 5.10 p.m.; & 4.10 p.m. on sundays. Postal orders are issued here, but not paid. Clovelly is the nearest money order office

National School, for 60 children; average attendance, 41; Mrs. Mary Ann Kallaway, mistress

BUCKS MILLS.

Cary-Elwes Richard James J.P. Walland Cary
Hughes Rev. David M.A. Vicarage

COMMERCIAL.

Davey William, farmer & builder, North Betworthy
Dark Matilda (Mrs.), shopkeeper
Harding John, farmer, Walland
Heywood George, farmer, Watershute
Jewell Richd. fishmonger, West Bucks
Kellaway Henry, fishmonger
Smale Elizabeth Ann (Mrs.), aparts
Warmington William, farmer & cattle dealer, Bucks Barton

BUCK'S CROSS.

Crews Simon, farmer
Dark James, farmer
Davey Robert, mason
Dayman John Henry, blacksmith
Jenn William, shopkeeper & assistant overseer, Post office
Steer Henry, carpenter & farmer

Bucks Mills village.

Winding steps to the harbour.

CLOVELLY is a picturesque village on the sea coast of Bideford bay, extending down the cliffs through a ravine to the quay or harbour, and is a parish 11 miles west from Bideford station on the Torrington branch of the London and South Western railway, and 5 east-north-east from Hartland, in the North Western division of the county, Hartland hundred, Bideford petty sessional division, union and county court district, rural deanery of Hartland, archdeaconry of Barnstaple and diocese of Exeter. The church of All Saints is an ancient building of stone in mixed styles, consisting of chancel, nave, north aisle, south porch of Norman date and an embattled western tower containing 5 bells, 3 of which were cast in 1758: there are several memorials to the Cary family, one of which has been curiously imposed upon another of earlier date; this is a large slab about 6 feet by 2, incised with a tall floriated cross, and marginal inscription, now much worn, to Hugh Myghellstowe or Michelstowe, ob. 1488: on the head of the cross has been placed the brass effigy of a man in armour, and over his head an inscription to Robert Cary esq. ob. 15 June, 1540; on the floor of the sacrarium are two small brass effigies of knights in armour, the larger of which has been assumed to represent Sir William Cary kt. killed at Tewkesbury, May 4, 1471, and the other Robert Cary esq. his son, ob. 1545; there is also a monument to Robert Cary esq. ob. 1586; a brass inscribed to George Cary esq. ob. 10 July, 1601; William Cary J.P. ob. 1652; Sir Robert Cary kt. ob. 1675, and other memorials to George Cary S.T.P. dean of Exeter, ob. Feb. 2, 1680; Sir George Cary kt. ob. 6 Jan. 1684-5, and several other members of this family: there are also monuments to the Williams family and a memorial window to Sir James Williams, erected by his daughters: the east window is a memorial to the late Nevile Fane esq. and the west window to the late Rev. William Harrison M.A. rector here 1883-99: the font, a very ancient work and supposed to be Saxon, is in a good state of preservation; a new organ was erected in 1090 at a cost of £300: in May, 1893, a brass was placed in the chancel to the memory of the Rev. Charles Kingsley M.A. rector of Eversley and canon of Westminster, the distinguished poet, preacher and novelist, who died 23 Jan. 1875; the church was restored in 1866, and has 350 sittings. The register dates from the year 1686. The living is a rectory, net yearly value £260, with residence, in the gift of Mrs. Hamlyn, and held since 1899 by the Rev. Thomas Leonard Vowe Simkin M.A. of St. John's College, Cambridge. The late Rev. Charles Kingsley spent a portion of his boyhood at Clovelly, of which his father was rector for four years. There is a Wesleyan Methodist chapel in the village, and a Bible Christian chapel, built in 1859, on the borders of the parish. The village, approached from Bideford through a wood known as the "Hobby," is romantic and singular in its arrangement, being built in a ravine, up which the narrow street is carried almost by a succession of steps; it is much celebrated for its herring fishery. On the south side of the village are the remains of a circular encampment, called "Clovelly Dykes," an ancient British encampment, situated on very high ground, commanding the only practicable coast road in this part of the country: it consists of three trenches or dykes, inclosing a quadrilateral area, 360 feet in length and 300 in breadth. The scenery in this neighbourhood is strikingly beautiful, some fresh prospect presenting itself at every turn: the Wilderness especially is a delightful walk, and at the termination of the grounds are Gallantry Bower and Mouth Mill, the latter exhibiting curious geological contortions and remarkable arrangements of strata, where the rock scenery, surrounded by majestic woods, is extremely fine. The hills around Clovelly rise in successive elevations, and between the different ranges and spurs are densely wooded glens, through which numerous streamlets make their way: to the west, along the shores of Bideford bay, the Carboniferous rocks extend in dark heavy masses; and to the north the coast of Pembrokeshire can be made out, with Lundy island in mid-channel. Here is a Reading Room, with a library of about 500 volumes. Clovelly Court, near the village, built in 1780, is the seat of Fredk. Hamlyn esq. D.L., J.P. who is lord of the manor and sole landowner. The soil is various; the subsoil is clay and rock. The chief crops are oats and wheat. The area is 3,395 acres of land and 100 of foreshore; rateable value, £2,428; the population in 1901 was 621.

Parish Clerk, Caleb Littlejohns.

Post, M. O. & T. O., T. M. O., S. B., Express Delivery & Parcels & Annuity & Insurance Office.—Mrs. Grace Pengilly Howard, sub-postmistress. Leters from Bideford received at 9.25 a.m. & dispatched at 4.30 p.m. & 3.30 p.m. on sunday

Wall Letter Box, Turnpike Gate, cleared at 5 p.m.; sundays, 4 p.m

Life Boat Station, Beach, Robert Badcock, coxswain

Coast Guard Station & Rocket Life Saving Apparatus, Dan Pearce, chief officer & 6 men

A School Board of 5 members was formed Feb. 12, 1873; James Lott, Wrinklebury, clerk to the board

Board School (mixed), built in 1872, & since enlarged, for 159 children; average attendance, 91; John Hobbs Seldon, master

Carriers.—Eli Braund & Frederick Robins, to Bideford, tues. thurs. & sat

Mail wagonette daily, 5 p.m. sundays 4 p.m. from Turnpike gate, taking passengers

Andrew Thomas, Lower Slerra
Bakewell Misses
Bate Mrs. Terranova cottage
Burnard John
Hamlyn Frederick esq. D.L., J.P. Clovelly court
Hamlyn Mrs. Clovelly court
Jewell William
Mills Richard
Simkin Rev. Thomas Leonard Vowe M.A. Rectory
Walker Robert

COMMERCIAL.

Allen Thomas, farmer, Blagdon
Andrew William, farmer, Burnstone
Bailey Catherine (Miss), apartments
Baker John, farm bailiff to Frederick Hamlyn esq. J.P. Court farm
Bartlett Thomas, farmer, Hugglepit
Bate Charles Hy. master mariner
Bate Charlotte (Mrs.), apartments
Bate William, apartments
Becklake James, farmer, Eastacott
Beer Mary (Mrs.), farmr. Low. Slerra
Beer William, head gamekeeper to F. Hamlyn esq. D.L., J.P
Berriman James, New Inn hotel
Braund Eli, carrier, Wrinklebury
Bragg Thomas, farmer, & carriages on hire, Lower Slerra
Bromell John, farmer, Stetworthy
Burman Harriet (Mrs.), apartments
Burman Richard, blacksmith, Slerra
Burrow Joseph, farmer, Higworthy
Cann Samuel, builder, brick, lime & coal merchant & ship owner; & at Hartland
Cleave Thomas, farmer, East Dyke
Cruse T. (Miss), farmer, West Dyke
Elliott William, farmer, Slade
Harding Mary A. (Mrs.), apartments
Harris Mary Ann (Mrs.), laundress
Heard Eleanor (Miss), apartments
Howard Grace Pengilly (Mrs.), grocr. Post office
Jeffery Elizabeth (Mrs.), apartments
Jennings Thomas, farmer, Slerra
Jennings William, farmer, Buscott
Jewell John, farmer, Wrinklebury
Jewell John B. shopkeeper
Lewis Emma (Mrs.), apartments
Littlejohns Caleb, shoe maker, Slerra
Lott James, estate carpenter & clerk to the School Board, Wrinklebury
Marshall Charles, master mariner
May John, carpenter & farmer, Dyke
Mills Mary (Mrs.), apartments
Moss Capt. John, harbour master & smack owner
Moss John, jun. coal dlr. & aprtmnts

(Continued p. 76.)

New Lodge, Clovelly Court.

The view down the street, *c.* 1887.

Trawlers in the harbour; the old roofless house in the background was the home of the Ship-wrecked Mariners' Society which was founded after a fishing disaster in 1821 in which 31 fishermen lost their lives; there was a further disaster in 1838 in which 21 lives were lost.

Crazed Kate's cottage, *c.* 1885.

Boats in the harbour, 1920. Fred Shackson is the man in the boat.

Harbour steps.

The yard at the back of the Red Lion Hotel. Roland Hortop (Snr.) is the man with the donkey. The fisherman at the top of the steps is 'Old' Steve Headon; the young lady is Molly Moss, the landlord's daughter. The photograph was taken in 1906.

The Harbour.

The RNLI Life Boat – The *Elinor Roget*. The crew, left to right: Fred Headon (bow man), Richard Cruse, Charlie Headon, Bert Braund, George Lamey, Thomas Pengelly (coxswain), Roland Hortop, Alfred Braund (second coxswain). Men standing, left to right: Charles Shackson, James Whitfield, Jack Harris, Steven Headon, Joe Dunn, William Badcock, William Hamlyn, Cecil Braund, Mr Steel (secretary), *c*. 1920.

Clovelly fishermen, *c*. 1880.

Clovelly fishermen in 1903. Left to right: Sam Shackson, Tom Jenn, 'Ganger' Harris, William Moss, William Bate, Jim Jenn, John Cruse, 'Old' Steve Headon, Robert Hodge, Amrose Pennington, Jamin Smale, Richard Cruse, Richard Foley, Richard Headon.

The 'Look-out' looking from Star Cottage in 1890.

Herring fishing 1917: the man in the foreground is William Jeffrey and the woman is Irene Perham.

Making lobster pots 1911. Left to right: Richard Cruse, Thomas Cruse (Snr.), Thomas Cruse (Jnr.), James Cruse and Oscar Abbot.

Clovelly donkeys, photographed from the archway of the Red Lion, 1920.

The beast of burden.

The post office in 1890; Mrs Grace Pengilley Howard was the sub-postmistress in 1902.

(Continued from p. 65.)

Moss Mary (Mrs.), apartments
Moss Sarah (Mrs.), apartments
Paddon Richard, carpenter & farmer, Lower Slerra
Parsons Fanny (Mrs.), laundress
Parsons Joseph, farmer, High. Slerra
Pedler Elizabeth (Mrs.), apartments
Pengilly Elizabeth (Mrs.), aprtmnts
Pengilly Sarah (Mrs.), apartments
Pennington Grace (Mrs.), apartments
Pickard Susan (Mrs.), grocer & drapr
Reading Room & Library (Mrs. Hamlyn, hon. sec)
Robins Frederick, carrier & farmer, Wrinklebury
Robins Henry, farmer, Clifford
Shepherd Catherine (Mrs.), apartments, Rose cottage
Slee John, farmer, Downland
Smale Mary (Mrs.), apartments
Tuke Harry, head gardener to F. Hamlyn esq
Vanstone James, farmer, Burford
Vine Lydia (Mrs.), Red Lion hotel
Walker Robert F.R.C.S. & L.R.C.P. Edin. surgeon & admiralty surgeon & agent & surgeon to the coastguard
Whitefield James, carpenter & boat builder
Woodley George, stud groom to F. Hamlyn esq. D.L., J.P. Clovelly crt

The arrival of the Royal Mail – Mr Martin and donkey, 1920.

The New Inn in 1870 – an early view down the main street.

GEORGEHAM is a parish and village, pleasantly seated on the Bristol Channel, 3 miles north-west from Braunton station on the Ilfracombe branch of the London and South Western railway, 8 west-north-west from Barnstaple and 7½ south-west from Ilfracombe, in the North Western division of the county, Braunton hundred and petty sessional division, Barnstaple union and county court district, rural deanery and archdeaconry of Barnstaple and diocese of Exeter. The church of St. George is a building of stone in the Gothic style, consisting of chancel, nave, south aisle, south porch and an embattled western tower containing 6 bells, all cast by Abel Rudhall, of Gloucester, in 1748, except the second, which dates from 1765: immediately in front of the chancel is an altar tomb with the recumbent cross-legged effigy of a knight in hauberk and mail armour, covered with a cyclas, or long-skirted garment, and carrying a shield; the figure is supposed to represent Sir Mauger St. Aubyn (de St. Albino), ob. 22 Edward I. (1294): there are other memorials to the family of Harriss: the stained east window is a memorial to the Rev. Francis Hole, formerly rector here, and there is a sculptured reredos by Hems, of Exeter: the organ was erected in 1881 as a memorial to Frances, wife of the Rev. F. Hole: in 1876-7 the church was almost entirely rebuilt under the direction of the late Mr. Fowler, architect, of Louth, at a cost of £3,500, chiefly defrayed by T. Hole esq. and his relatives: in the churchyard is a tomb to Simon Gould and Julian, his wife, who died in 1817, in the 101st year of their respective ages, and the 75th year of their married life: there are 300 sittings. The register of baptisms dates from the year 1540; marriages and burials, 1538. The living is a rectory, net yearly value £398, with residence and 23 acres of glebe, in the gift of trustees and held since 1886 by the Rev. William Henry George Francis Hole. The Baptist chapel, erected in 1884, has sittings for 120 persons. The charities include one of £400, left by Mr. William Vellacotts, half of the interest of which is applied to the education of poor children, the other half being distributed yearly amongst the poor: the interest of Chugg's charity of £400, amounting to £13 10s. is distributed by the rector and churchwardens on New Year's day to the poor of the parish. Earl Fortescue is lord of the manor. Major Richard Horwood Dunning, of Winkleigh, Mrs. Dennis and Mrs. Incledon-Webber, of St. Brannock's, Braunton, are the chief landowners. The soil is light; subsoil, sandy. The crops are barley and oats, with a small quantity of wheat and oats. The area is 4,160 acres of land and 174 of foreshore, rateable value, £4,885; the population in 1891 was 747.

CROYDE is a hamlet, 1 mile south-west, and from its pleasant situation is now much frequented as a health resort and for sea-bathing, and a number of lodging houses have consequently been built. The chapel of St. Mary Magdalen, erected in 1874, at a cost of £500, is a plain building of stone, consisting of chancel and nave, with an attached schoolroom: there are 150 sittings: divine service is held here every Sunday by the rector of Georgeham. The Baptist chapel, erected in 1882, affords sittings for 150 persons, and has a Sunday school and burial ground attached. A rocket life-saving apparatus is kept here, in connection with which there is telephonic communication to Ilfracombe and other places on the coast.

NORTH BUCKLAND, 1 mile east, DARRACOTT, three-quarters south-east, and PUTTSBOROUGH, 1 mile west, are in this parish.

Sexton, John Thomas.

Post & M. O. O., S. B. & Annuity & Insurance Office.—Mrs. Annie Spencer, sub-postmistress. Letters through Braunton R.S.O. North Devon arrive at 7.30 a.m.; dispatched at 12.15 & 6.5 p.m. The nearest telegraph office is at Croyde, 1½ miles distant

Post & T. O. & Express Delivery Office, Croyde, with telephonic communication to Barnstaple. — Arthur Gammon, sub-postmaster. Letters arrive from Braunton R.S.O. North Devon at 7.40 a.m.; dispatched at 11.45 a.m. & 5.35 p.m. week days only. Postal orders are issued here, but not paid. Georgeham is the nearest money order office

Wall Letter Box, at Croyde Sands, cleared at 11.15 a.m. & 5.5 p.m

Schools.

School (mixed), rebuilt, with master's residence, in 1868, & partly endowed by funds mentioned above; these will hold about 150 children; average attendance, 96; Clement Richards, master; Miss Smale, infants' mistrss

Carriers to Barnstaple—William Shapland, fri

From Croyde to Barnstaple—John Lovering, fri

Henry Newcombe, police constable

Putsborough Manor, Georgeham.

Bee boles in a wall at Georgeham. Built to take the bee skips made of straw, before wood hives became common, *c.* 1911.

The village, c. 1910.

Croyde village: the Carpenter's Arms in background.

Croyde village.

Hartland Abbey.

Kelly says of Hartland (or Harton) '... by repute a prescriptive borough, is a small town and extensive parish, on the coast of Bude bay, 13 miles west-by-south from the Bideford station on the Torrington branch of the London and South Western railway ....'. Of Hartland Abbey 'that it was founded in the reign of Henry II by Geoffrey de Dinham as a house of Austin Canons in place of a college of secular canons.... The foundation was confirmed between 1157 and 1184 by Bartholomew, Bishop of Exeter....'. The site of the abbey is seated in a beautifully-wooded valley and surrounded by a park which is well stocked with deer, and traversed by a trout stream. The mansion, erected about 1779 incorporates in the right wing a portion of the abbey buildings; the hall, 72 feet in length, and the cloisters, at that time perfect and unaltered, were partially destroyed, but a portion of the cloister was retained and included in the basement ....'

Fore Street West.

Hartland.

St John's, The Square.

'St Johns – a chapel of ease, built in 1839, on the site of the old town hall, consists of a chancel, nave and porch on the east side, over which there is a turret containing a clock and one bell: it was thoroughly restored in 1882 at a cost of £200, and has two stained windows; there are sittings for 300 persons. There are Wesleyan and Congregational chapels in the town; Wesleyan chapels at Meddon and Elmscott, and Bible Christian chapels at Hartland, Eddistone and Harbour.... An annual market for sheep and cattle is held here on the second Saturday in March; and fairs for cattle are held on Easter Wednesday and September 25th, and at the West Country Inn, also in this parish, on the first Wednesday in August, and on the third Thursday in October. The Hartland and Clovelly Cottage Garden Society, established in 1857, has an exhibition here on the last Wednesday in July, annually ....'

West Country Inn. James Woodley was landlord in 1902.

The Chapel.

Stoke Church, Hartland.

Stoke, Hartland.

HEANTON PUNCHARDON is a parish and village, standing on an eminence north of the Taw estuary, with a station at Wrafton in this parish on the North Devon branch of the London and South Western railway, and is 4½ miles west-north-west from Barnstaple, in the North Western division of the county, Braunton hundred and petty sessional division, Barnstaple union and county court district, and in the rural deanery and archdeaconry of Barnstaple and diocese of Exeter. The church of St. Augustine is an ancient building of stone in the Early English style, consisting of chancel and nave, north aisle, south porch and an embattled western tower with pinnacles, containing 6 bells, cast by Taylor, of Oxford, but undated: in the church are several monuments to the ancient family of Bassett, including Sir Robert Bassett kt. ob. 11 Nov. 1641, and Elizabeth (Peryam), his wife, ob. 1635; Col. Arthur Bassett, their eldest son, ob. 7 Jan. 1672, and William, their second son, ob. 7 May, 1674; there are others to John Bassett esq. ob. 1 August, 1660; Susanna (Bluett), his wife, ob. 22 April, 1662; John Bassett esq. ob. 13 May, 1686, and Elizabeth (Acland), his wife, ob. 6 Nov. 1683: in the chancel is a canopied altar-tomb, with a feathered arch; in the spandrils are the intertwined letters R. C. and above the cornice are the arms of the Coffin family, supported by an angel; the inscription is lost, but the tomb is assumed to commemorate Richard Coffin esq. ob. 16th century, and his wife, a daughter of Sir Richard Chudleigh kt.: a tablet was erected in 1891, by the rector and fellows of Exeter College, Oxford, to the Rev. George Hakewill, archdeacon of Surrey and chaplain to Prince Charles, son of James I. ob. 1649, aged 72: the church was restored in 1889-90, at a cost of £916, the tower being restored and the bells rehung, at the expense of Sir William Williams bart.; the old pews have been replaced by modern seats, and a stained window inserted at the east end: the oaken pulpit and lectern are new: the church affords 230 sittings. The register dates from the year 1584. The living is a rectory, net yearly value £307, with residence and 38 acres of glebe, in the gift of Frank Sellwood and the trustees of Binwood Sellwood, and held since 1887 by the Rev. Charles Edward Lamb M.A. of Corpus Christi college, Cambridge, and surrogate. The charities are of £20 yearly value. Heanton Court, now a farm-house, once the seat of the Punchardon family, forms a conspicuous object from Barnstaple bridge. Sir William Robert Williams bart. of Upcott, is lord of the manor and chief landowner, and the manor of West Ashford, a large demesne, is also his property. The soil is loamy; the subsoil, clayey. The chief crops are wheat, potatoes and pasturage. The area is 2,427 acres of land, 15 of water, 117 of tidal water and 602 of foreshore; rateable value, £3,246; the population in 1901 was 404.

The hamlets are—CHIVENOR, three-quarters of a mile south; WRAFTON, three-quarters of a mile west; and WEST ASHFORD, 1½ miles east.

Post Office, Wrafton (Railway Sub-Office. Letters should have R.S.O. North Devon added).—John Sanders, sub-postmaster. Letters arrive at 5.55 a.m.; dispatched at 7.25 p.m. Postal orders are issued here, but not paid. Braunton is the nearest money order & telegraph office, 1 mile distant

A School Board of 5 members was formed November 24, 1874, for the united district of Heanton Punchardon & Ashford

Board School (mixed), built in 1877, for 110 children; average attendance, 70; Henry Westacott, master

Railway Station, Wrafton, John Andrews, station master

The Rectory and Church, Heanton.

HEANTON PUNCHARDON.

Pitfield John, Wrafton house
Chugg Joshua, farmer, Eastacombe
Dunn Jeremiah, farmer, Heanton ct
Westacott Henry, schoolmaster & assistant overseer & clerk to the Parish Council

WRAFTON.

Abbot John, under steward to Sir W. R. Williams bart. Manor house
Lamb Rev. Chas. Edwd. M.A. Rectory
Ayre William, farmer, Part of Glebe
Clarke Thos. shopkpr. & master marinr
Corney William, blacksmith
Corney William, master mariner
Drake Henry, master mariner
Drake Henry, jun. master mariner
Hernaman Richard, farmer, Hart farm
Hernaman Wm. farmer, Mainstone
Newcombe Frank, market gardener
Newcombe Hy. Exeter inn, & farmer
Reed Jas. Darracott, farmr. Manor fm
Reed William, farmer, Poyer's farm
Rodd William, thatcher
Sanders John, tailor, Post office
Skinner Chas. Napier, farmr. Marsh frm
Stevens William, mariner
Tarr Wm. miller (water), Heanton mls

WEST ASHFORD BARTON.

Corney George, undertaker
Saunder Edwin T. farmer

CHIVENOR.

Berry Thomas, farmer
Reed John, farmer

Chamber Farm – reputed to be haunted:

'Tis said the gentle Lady Grey
Once stayed where champernounes held sway,
In this ancestral Hall;
And as she wandered through the glade,
Little thought she the cruel blade
On her fair neck would fall.

Wrafton village.

Celebrations to mark the opening of the railway.

Kelly's Directory describes Ilfracombe as a 'watering-place, seaport, market town and parish, and was a terminal station on a branch from Barnstaple of the London and South Western Railway, 226 miles from London . . . the extension of the S Western line from Barnstaple to Ilfracombe was completed in July 1874.. . . Steam packets also ply during the season to Lynmouth, Bristol, Padstow, Hayle and Swansea. This town, as a watering place, is of rising importance, the warmth, salubrity and equable character of its atmosphere rendering it a favourable resort, for invalids and other visitors; the average winter temperature is about one degree higher than that of Torquay.. . . The rate of mortality is very low, the average, including visitors, being 15 in 1000; it is sheltered by the eminence known as Capstone Hill, 156 feet in height on the north shore, and Lantern Hill, overlooking the harbour between the town and the Bristol Channel. The town stands on a stratum of slate rock, intersected by veins of quartz at an angle of nearly 45°; hence the drainage is perfect, and in a few hours after heavy rains, the town and walks become dry. It formerly consisted of only one irregular street, nearly a mile in length, but has . . . been much altered and extended and now contains many thoroughfares; terraces and detached villas have been built, chiefly for the convenience of summer visitors, and around the Capstone walks have been constructed.'

Church Street, Ilfracombe, *c.* 1870.

Old Fore Street.

High Street in 1891.

The old Lamb Inn, before demolition; it was rebuilt in 1893 as the Lamb Hotel, High Street.

Barclays Bank, 1898.

The High Street in 1902.

Parrett's Stores, *c.* 1897. Joseph Parrett & Son had two shops in 1902 – one was a grocery and provision dealers and agent for W.A. Gilby Ltd., wine and spirit merchants at No. 127 High Street; the other way – a fruiterers at No. 7 High Street.

A back entrance in Market Street.

Mr Day's butcher's shop, No. 121b High Street.

William Myatt's Circulating Library, on the corner of Northfield Road, *c.* 1899; it became the Gas showroom in 1977.

John Henry Smith's butcher's shop, No. 118c High Street; this photograph was taken *c.* 1890.

Reed's Hairdresser and Tobacconist, High Street.

W. Phillips, Fish & Game dealer, *c.* 1890.

Fore Street – Montebello's Hotel, pre-1892.

BOOK HERE
COLWILLS
COACHES
LYNTON
LYNTON
BOOK HERE
ONLY

Sam Colwill (with the beard) was the coach operator; he was also once Town Mayor. His son, Tom Colwill, was the driver, and the guard – also in a top hat – was Bert Gear. Colwill's office was next door to the Queens Hotel at No. 96 High Street.

The Lizzie, a fishing boat in harbour.

The *F.A.M.E.* built at Plymouth in 1800 and later owned by Barnstaple and Braunton owners. Her remains are now in the River Parret. The ketch *Georgina*, 52 tons, built at Saul in 1869 and owned in that area throughout her life.

Thomas Rudd and a boy, with nets.

The Harbour.

'The harbour is formed by a natural basis, surrounded and nearly enclosed by rocks; at the entrance is a pier, originally erected by the Bourchiers, Earls of Bath,. . . it was lengthened, partly rebuilt and enlarged in 1766, by Sir Bourchier Wrey, bart., M.P. then Lord of the manor; in the year 1823 it sustained considerable damage, but was further enlarged and repaired by his son in 1824, and completed in 1829 by Sir Bourchier Palk Wrey, bart., late Lord of the Manor . . . a low water jetty was constructed in 1873. The ancient chapel of St Nicholas (the patron saint of sailors) situated on the Lantern Rock, at the entrance to the harbour . . . has been converted into a lighthouse.' Kelly goes on to name and describe all the churches, chapels and main hotels in the town, also the Town Hall and the Market House which were built in 1862.

Watching the paddle-steamers. Left to right: *Lorna Doone* (Edwards Robertson & Co.). At the stone bench: *Westward Ho!* (P. & A. Campbell Ltd); *Brodick Castle* (The Bristol & Ilfracombe Steam Ship Co.); *Earl of Dunraven* (under charter to Edwards, Robertson). At the outside berth: Left to right: *Brighton* (Pockett's Bristol Channel Steam Packet Co. Ltd); *Ravenswood* (P. & A. Cambell Ltd). This photograph was taken after mid-August 1894 by E.D. Percival, Art Gallery – Nos 4 & 5 High Street, Ilfracombe.

The *Alexandra*, photographed in 1883, leaving harbour; she was owned by C.E. Daniel.

Steam ships, *c.* 1900–1903. Left to right: Tug *Privateer*; PS *Brighton*; PS *Ravenswood*; PS *Scotia*; PS *Westward Ho!*; PS *Lorna Doone*. Printed and published as a Mammoth Postcard by Ingram Clarke & Co. Ltd, Ilfracombe & Bristol.

The Pavilion – built in 1888.

'The Victoria Promenade, at the foot of the Capstone, erected in 1888 at a cost of £4,000 . . . is a large building of iron and glass 200 ft long, and 35 ft wide, with three entrances, a central dome and a verandah in front; the interior, which contains an orchestra, is filled with graceful palms and climbing plants, and there are attached cloak and retiring rooms'. (Kelly.)

INSTOW is a parish and village, at the confluence of the rivers Taw and Torridge, immediately opposite the town of Appledore, and on the high road from Bideford to Barnstaple, having a station on the North Devon extension of the London and South Western railway, and is 6 miles west from Barnstaple, 3 north-east from Bideford and 217½ from London, in the North Western division of the county, Fremington hundred, Braunton petty sessional division, Barnstaple union, Bideford county court district, rural deanery and archdeaconry of Barnstaple and diocese of Exeter. Instow is much frequented in summer as a watering place, and a vessel from hence sails every Thursday to Lundy Island in the Bristol channel. The church of St. John the Baptist is an ancient building of stone in the Gothic style, consisting of chancel, nave, north aisle, transept, south porch and an embattled western tower, containing 3 bells, of which the first has a legend in Old English letters; the others are dated 1694 and 1682: the church was thoroughly restored in 1875 at a cost of £1,400, and a new vestry was built in 1880: there are 300 sittings. The register dates from the year 1717. The living is a rectory, net yearly value £[illegible], including 31 acres of glebe, with residence, in the gift of A. L. Christie esq. and held since 1893 by the Rev. Samuel Charles Haines Ph.D. of the University of Rostock. Here is a Wesleyan chapel. Joan Tucker's charity, of £2 yearly, is distributed among the poor. Augustus Langham Christie esq. of Tapeley Park, Westleigh, who is lord of the manor and Miss Arundell Yeo, of Fremington House, are the chief landowners. The soil is light loam; subsoil, clay. The area is 1,698 acres of land, 1 of water, 54 of tidal water and 303 of foreshore; rateable value, £2,973; the population in 1901 was 634.

Sexton, John Braunton.

Post, M. O. & T. O., T. M. O., S. B., Express & Parcel Delivery, Annuity & Insurance Office (Railway Sub-Office. Letters should have R.S.O. North Devon added).—Thomas Molland, postmaster. Letters arrive per railway, at 5.45 & 11.20 a.m. & 4.55 p.m.; sundays, 5.45 a.m.; dispatched at 9.40 a.m. & 2.5 & 7.35 p.m.; sundays, 7.35 p.m

Wall Letter Boxes, Lane end, cleared at 9.5 a.m. & 1.20 & 7 p.m.; sunday, 8.30 a.m.; Instow Town, cleared at 8.40 a.m.; 12.50 & 6.35 p.m. week days only; Worlington house, 7.15 a.m. & 6 p.m. week days only

A School Board of 5 members was formed Nov. 23, 1874; F. Lee, East Leigh, clerk to the board

Board School (mixed), erected in 1888, for 100 children; average attendance, 87; John Whitlock, master

Police Station, Lane end, John Whitefield, constable

Ferry-boats cross to Appledore as often as required

Railway Station, Frederick Field, station master

Instow from Appledore.

Ladies at a Unionist garden meeting at Strandfield – 24 July 1912.

The same Conservative Garden Fête, held where the Commodore Hotel now stands. Beatrice Pedlar (née Way) is the maid; she was in service at the Rectory.

PRIVATE RESIDENTS.

Ayerst Mrs. Riverside house
Dering Mrs. Edgar, 7 Bath terrace
Dorsett George, Strandfield
Everett Charles Edwin, The Verne
Fraser Mrs. Little hill
Gorton Gilbert B.A. Little hill
Gough Mrs. Instow town
Gregory Mrs. The Cottage
Haines Rev. Samuel Charles Ph.D. (rector), Rectory
Hayes Mrs. 2 Bath terrace
Hinchliff Mrs. Worlington house
Hulton Mrs
Hulton Mrs. Frank
Jones-Bateman Rev. Cecil M.A.Hillsly
Lemarchand Mrs. 3 Victoria terrace
Lock Miss, Lewismead
Lock William Henry, Springfield
Loveband Mrs. Newton house
Mallett Miss, Marine cottage
Molloy Col. Edward C.B. Fair view
O'Brien Lieut.-Col. Joseph,The Dunes
Patch James, 3 Bath terrace
Powell Miss, Round house
Pridham Col. Frederick, Rose cottage
Rand Mrs. The Quay
Turner Henry, The Barton
White Rev. John BennyB.A.Instow ho
White Mrs. 5 Bath terrace
Whyte Miss, 1 Victoria terrace

COMMERCIAL.

Anstey Thomas, farmer, South Yeo
Braunton John, hind to H. Turner esq. Glebe cottage
Burnacle Maria (Mrs.), apartments, Galsworthy house
Bellew William, farmer, Orchard farm
Carter Mary (Mrs.), farmr.Bickleton
Cleverdon Thos. aparts. Sea View ho
Connebear John Brayley, Marine hotel, family & posting house; charming situation, overlooking rivers Taw & Torridge & Bay; private lawn with sea wall; near railway station & central for all places of interest in North Devon; within easy distance of the North Devon golf links & cricket ground; good boating & bass fishing
Dean William, tailor, Lane end
Dennis Frederick, farmer, Fullincott
Dobbs Albert Reginald, watch maker, The Quay
Dobbs John, aparts. 2 Victoria ter
Easterbrook Wm. Atwill, New inn
England Jonathan,bootmaker & assistant overseer
Farleigh John Kenworthy, grocer, The Quay
Field Frederick, station master, 2 South view
Gayton Wm. thatcher, Lyndale villas
Hare John, apartments, Marine ter
Hoyles David Thorn, blacksmith & taxidermist, Instow town
Instow Tennis & Croquet Club (A. G. Schneider, hon. sec)
Johns Richd. ferryman, The Quay
Jones Edward A. butcher
Joslin James, farmer, Raddey farm
Joslin John, farmer, Huish farm
Knott Mary Ann (Miss), apartments, Myrtle villa
Lock Thomas, shopkpr. Lane end
Lock William Henry, land agent & surveyor, Springfield
Marshall Henrietta (Mrs.), apartments, Lane end
Matthews William, tailor, The Quay
Molland Helen (Miss), apartments, Marine terrace
Molland Thos. stationer, Post office
Nation William, butcher & farmer
North Devon Cricket Club & Ground (Rev. J. B. White B.A. hon. sec)
Parkhouse Emma (Mrs.), apartments, 4 Victoria terrace
Parochial Lending Library (James Patch, hon. sec)
Pickard John, carpenter, Instow twn
Pidler Alexander, farmer, Down farm
Pidler Christopher, refreshment rms. & shopkeeper, Lane end
Pidler John, mason, Lane end
Pidler Wm. Hy. Fishley, coal dealer
Rattenberry John Littlejohns, apartments, Bar view
Sexton Ernest, mason, Lane end
Shackson Joseph Ernest, mason, Lane end
Smith Ernest Alfred, bakr.Marine ter
Trick William Evans, apartments, Marine terrace
Tucker William Henry, boarding ho. 2 Galsworthy house
Turner Henry, farmer, The Barton
Vanstone Elizh. Grace (Mrs.), aparts
WhitefieldJn.police constable,Lane end
Worth James, apartments
Yeo Henry, carpenter & wheelwright

The sea wall, Instow. It is believed that the crowd were watching the Regatta in 1914.

Instow from the sands.

LUNDY ISLAND, situated in the Bristol channel, 15 miles north-west from Clovelly, constitutes a parish in the North Western division of the county, petty sessional division, union and county court district of Bideford, hundred of Braunton, rural deanery of Hartland, archdeaconry of Barnstable and diocese of Exeter; it is 3 miles nautical, or nearly 3½ statute miles in length, by 1 nautical, or rather more than 1 statute mile in greatest breath, but being very irregular in outline, does not average more than ½ of a mile in breadth, giving an area of about 1.500 acres; the whole, together with the sea surrounding it for 3 miles, from low water mark, is included in the port of Barnstaple; the nearest railway station is Westward Ho! on the Bideford and Westward Ho! Railway, opened in May, 1901; the island is surrounded by lofty and inaccessible rocks, except on the eastern side, where it can be approached only by a very small entrance: on this side is the roadstead, which is much frequented by outward bound vessels and pilot and tug boats, and affords to craft entering or leaving the Bristol channel the only shelter from westerly gales: communication with the mainland is secured by means of a sailing vessel every Thursday from Instow, by which the weekly mails are conveyed, and, during the summer months only, a steamer runs from Ilfracombe three or four times a week, as well as occasionally from Barnstaple and Bideford. The steamer "Devonia," plying between Bideford and Bristol, calls at the island when required. The ancient chapel of St. Helen, with the annexed oratory of St. Anne, traditionally said to have been in use, at least for funeral services, in the reign of William III. has now been for many years a ruin. In 1889 the proprietor and his family erected an iron church, which was opened and licensed by the Bishop of Exeter, and affords 82 sittings: but in 1896-7, a permanent church of local granite was erected on an elevated site, at a cost of over £4,000, from designs by Mr. John Norton F.R.I.B.A. of London, and dedicated, like its predecessor, to St. Helen. It contains a fine reredos, with three marble panels, displaying, in high relief, representations of the "Passover," the "Scape goat in the Wilderness," and the "Last Supper"; this work, as well as the pulpit, font and a statue of St. Helen in a niche over the south-west entrance, being executed by Hems and Sons, of Exeter; the entire expense is borne by the rector, who has built the Church as a votive offering. The church, opened June, 1897, affords 164 sittings. No parish registers are known to exist; certainly none have been kept since the Reformation; births and deaths have been registered of late years by the registrar of the Hartland district. The living is a rectory, the patronage belonged in pre-Reformation times to Cleeve Abbey, in Somersetshire, but on the suppression of that house the patronage appears to have lapsed, and no appointment has ever since been made; the glebe, if any, passed to the owner of the island: the incumbency is in the gift of and has been held since 1864 by the Rev. Hudson Grosett Heaven M.A. of Trinity College, Oxford. There is an ancient burial ground attached to the remains of St. Helen's chapel, dating from the 13th century, the freehold of which appears to have passed into the possession of the landowner for the time being, on the suppression of monastic houses. There are no dissenting chapels of any kind. The ancient keep and other remains of Marisco Castle, dating from the time of Henry III. still exist, and there is a lighthouse and fog-signal station.

Two lighthouses have been erected by the Trinity House, one on the north end and the other on the west side of the island: these were completed about 1897.

Lloyd's have a signal station on the island. Telephonic communication with Barnstaple by day and Appledore by night, has also been established under Post Office control. The night telephone is for special use in case of wrecks and marine disaster requiring prompt assistance. The Rev. H. G. Heaven M.A. is lord of the manor (which retains very full manorial rights) and sole landowner. A handsome mansion was built here by the late William Hudson Heaven esq. The whole island, with the exception of about 60 acres, is held on lease for a term of 20 years by George John Taylor esq. who resides at Abbotsham Court, Bideford, and visits the island about every month. During the years 1899-1900 a large reservoir has been made for supplying the manor house with water. There is a large and well-appointed boarding-house, where visitors can be boarded "en pension"; terms can be obtained on application to Mrs. Pellman, Manor House, Lundy Island. There are also several cottages and a large luncheon room for visitors to the island, capable of holding 200 persons. There is very good fishing, and lobsters are caught in great quantities by Mr. Thomas, who will supply visitors with any quantity on application. Very good woodcock shooting can be had in winter. Mr. Taylor has arranged to run a steamer to Lundy during June, July, August and September, starting from Ilfracombe, Swansea and Sharpness, enabling visitors to stay on the island several hours. This is the only steamer allowed to land passengers on the island. The island, which is the sole property of the lord of the manor, is mainly formed of, and is famous for a very hard and durable granite, which furnished supplies for the construction, in 1864-70, of the Thames Embankment. Of the land, only about 200 acres are under cultivation, about 300 acres are maintained as permanent pasture, and the remainder is moorland. The soil is generally light, varying from light reddish loam to very light black sandy peat, overlying a varying subsoil of white and yellow clay or gravel. The chief crops are hay, oats, barley and roots. The island supports about 800 sheep and 100 beasts and horses, and is the nesting-place of millions of sea-birds of many different varieties. The area is about 1,500 acres, according to recent Ordnance survey, but has never been valued, and no rates are either levied or paid; there is 102 acres of foreshore in the parish; population is now (1901) about 25.

St Helens, Lundy.

South lighthouse and landing beach.

Wreck of HMS *Montagu*, 1906.

Outside the Marisco Tavern.

A group of sailors.

LYNMOUTH, so called from its situation at the confluence and mouth of the East and West Lyn, on the outskirts of Exmoor, is well known as a popular and beautiful watering-place, occupying a level site, near the seashore, at the entrance of an immense gorge, into which the magnificent ravine of the East Lyn and the densely-wooded but sequestered valley of the West Lyn abruptly descend, the twin streams, after heavy or long continued rains, assuming formidable proportions, and rush down to the sea with extraordinary speed and great uproar; within the circuit of a few miles inland there is every variety of hill and dale, with woody tracts and moorland of vast extent, and valleys of extreme beauty traversed by mountain streams dashing impetuously over their rock-strewn beds; the coast scenery here is also very fine and extensive: the Welsh coast is generally visible, and sometimes the hills of South Wales may be very distinctly made out. The nearest railway station is at Lynton, the terminus of the Lynton and Barnstaple railway, and about 1 mile distant. By an Order in Council, dated July 6, 1886, Lynmouth was ecclesiastically annexed to Countisbury, and is in the rural deanery of Sherwell and archdeaconry of Barnstaple. The church of St. John the Baptist, a chapel of ease to Countisbury, erected by voluntary contributions at a cost of about £2,000, is a building of stone in the Early English style, consisting of vaulted apsidal chancel, nave, south aisle, north porch and a western turret containing 2 bells: there are 220 sittings. The living is a perpetual curacy, annexed to the vicarage of Countisbury, and held since 1886 by the Rev. Albert Richards Hockley. There is also a Gospel mission hall. The Lyndale, Tors Park and Lyn Valley hotels afford every convenience for visitors. Here is also a public reading room; and a life-boat and life-saving rocket apparatus are maintained. Among the chief places of interest in the neighbourhood are Brendon Valley, Bossington hill, Culbone, Dunkery beacon, 1,668 feet above the sea level, Exmoor, about 14 miles square and largely uncultivated; Glenthorne, with a delightful coast path winding round the cliffs; Heddon's mouth, the entrance to a romantic valley, Lyndale, Lee bay, the Valley of Rocks, and the valleys of the West Lyn and Watersmeet. The Valley of Rocks is a wild region, in which the Castle rock, rising in a sheer precipice from the sea of 500 feet, is the most prominent feature. Watersmeet, up the East Lyn, which is crossed by rustic bridges, receives the Combe water; the narrow gorge is well wooded, and there is good fishing. A lighthouse was built in 1900 by the Trinity House authorities at a cost of £10,000, including the making of two miles of approach roads; the lighthouse stands about 200 feet above the sea, and has a keeper's residence attached. The population in 1901 was 402.

Post, M. O. & T. O., T. M. O., S. B., Express Delivery, Parcel & Annuity & Insurance Office.—Edward James Pedder, sub-postmaster. Letters arrive from Barnstaple at 8.55 a.m. & 6.43 p.m.; dispatched at 8.15 & 10.50 a.m. & 4.50 p.m.; sundays, received 9.45 a.m

PUBLIC ESTABLISHMENTS.

National Life Boat Institution, Lynmouth, Rev. A. R. Hockley, hon. sec

Public Reading Room, Lynmouth, John Elworthy, sec

Coast Guard Station, William Bromley, chief officer

Parish School (mixed), for 100 children; average attendance, 70; William Northcott, master

The Valley of the Rocks.

Lynton and Lynmouth.

Watersmeet Cottage.

Watersmeet.

Mr Darch, beside the Lyn.

The Rhenish tower, which was built by General Rowden around 1800, is an exact replica of a tower on the River Rhine in Germany. It was used as a beacon light for the harbour, and was destroyed in 1956.

Lynmouth from Mars Hill.

Mars Hill.

Lynmouth, *c.* 1900.

Lynmouth after the flood of August 1956.

The Town Hall.

LYNTON is a parish containing several hamlets, with a terminal station on the Lynton and Barnstaple railway now in course of construction; the village is 20 miles from each of the following towns, viz.:—Minehead, Barnstaple, South Molton and Ilfracombe, and stands on a wooded hill 900 feet in height, immediately above and connected by a cliff railway with Lynmouth, where the waters of the East and West Lyn unite and fall into the Bristol Channel, the scenery here, especially in the Valley of Rocks, being wild and romantic. Lynton is in the North Western division of the county, hundred of Shirwell, petty sessional division of Braunton, union and county court district of Barnstaple, rural deanery of Shirwell, archdeaconry of Barnstaple and diocese of Exeter.

Lynton has communication by coach with Ilfracombe and Minehead during the summer months. There are 7 hotels, viz.: "The Royal Castle," Lynton Cottage Private hotel (both in the same extensive and romantic grounds), the "Valley of Rocks," "the Crown," "the Imperial," "the Gobe" and "the Queen." The District Cottage Hospital, established in 1873, is a plain cottage building, enlarged in 1893 at a cost of £50, and is supported by voluntary contributions. The Foresters' Hall will seat about 300 persons. The Town Hall, erected and presented to the parish by Sir George Newnes bart. in 1900, is a building of stone and cost £20,000. The lift here, one of the longest and steepest of its kind, connecting Lynton with Lynmouth, was designed and built by Mr. Jones, of this town, and opened on Easter Monday, 1890. Lee Abbey is the residence of Frederick Charles Bailey esq. D.L., J.P. Mrs. Jeune, of Countisbury, is lady of the manor; the principal landowners are C. F. Bailey esq. J.P. Col. James Lean, Evan Browell Jeune esq. J.P. of Countisbury, Lady Carew and R. H. Taylor esq. The soil is light gravelly; subsoil, turf, in some parts rock; crops, oats and barley.

The Lyn.

Building the cliff railway between Lynton and Lynmouth, 1889. The railway was opened on Easter Monday 1890 by Sir George Newnes, who was also the benefactor. He performed the opening ceremony of this, the first such railway, based upon two platforms, each capable of carrying 20 passengers, connected by an endless cable passing round large pulley wheels, at the top and bottom of a double set of rails running sheer down a cliff face with a gradient of 1 in $1\frac{3}{4}$ for 900 ft, thus rising/falling 450 feet. The system remains unchanged; each platform has a very large tank underneath which is filled with water at the top and emptied out sufficiently at the bottom so that the top platform becomes heavier and pulls up the lower; each platform has automatic and emergency brakes. This scheme had been worked out by Bob Jones, a local engineer, around 1870 and only became a reality with the financial backing of Sir George, who is the gentleman on the left on the platform. In 1916/17, before Lynton Hill was tarmacked, cars were transported up or down the cliff railway by moving the carriages off the platforms, and it was said 'This is now the general practice as the damage done to the tyres in negotiating the steep Lynton Hill entails greater cost than the car fare by Cliff Railway'. The fares were: up 3*d*., down 2*d*., return 4*d*.; motor cars, 7*s*. 6*d*. for small cars, 10*s*. 6*d*. for large cars.

MORTEHOE (or Morte, as it is generally called) is a parish and village on the sea coast, with a station about 2 miles east of the village, on the Ilfracombe branch of the London and South Western railway, and 5 miles south-west from Ilfracombe, in the North Western division of the county, Braunton hundred and petty sessional division, Barnstaple union and county court district, rural deanery of Barnstaple and archdeaconry and diocese of Exeter.

By Local Government Board Order 15,900, a detached part of Mortehoe was transferred, for civil purposes, to Georgeham, March 24, 1884.

OSSABOROUGH, 2¼ miles south-east; SHAFTSBOROUGH, 2½ miles east; EASTACOTT, 2 miles south-east; and WOOLACOMBE, 1 mile south, are places in this parish.

Sexton, William Henry Watts.

The Chichester Hotel, Mortehoe; Charles Coles was 'mine host' in 1902. There appear to be ship's figureheads at either end of the garden seat.

The Rocket House. This is the building where the earliest rocket life-saving apparatus was kept. The record dates back to 1890; it is still operated by local volunteers today.

Towards Bull Point.

Bull Point Lighthouse, about 1 mile from the village, built in 1879 at a cost of about £7,000, has a triple-flashing half-minute white light, placed at an elevation of 154 feet above high water mark, and shows every 18 seconds three successive flashes of about two seconds' duration: it has a fixed red light to mark the position of "Morte Stone," a dangerous rock off the Point, and here also is a powerful fog-horn, worked by a pair of caloric engines, each of 2-horse power, and rocket life-saving apparatus with telephonic communication between Bull Point Lighthouse, Ilfracombe and Croyde. By arrangement with the Government telegraph department, casualties at sea can be telegraphed to owners of vessels and others from Bull Point.

'The Grange'. In 1902 it was 'Seaside Home for Ministers of all Denominations' with a Miss Knee as caretaker. It was founded by the Revd U.R. Thomas of Bristol.

'Glen Haven', Mortehoe. I can find no reference to this address in 1902 – possibly it was not built then.

Mortehoe village, *c.* 1880. The Wesleyan chapel is on the left (small spire); centre left is St Mary's Church; centre right is the board school.

St Mary's Church and the post office; George Conibear was sub-postmaster in 1902.

The church of St. Mary is an ancient edifice of stone in the Early English and Perpendicular styles, consisting of chancel, nave, south transept, north aisle, south porch and an embattled western tower containing a clock, placed in 1887, and 6 bells: the oldest portions of the existing structure are the nave and chancel; the latter, built in the 13th century, has a Transitional chancel arch; the north transept dates from the 15th century, or later; the tower, of the 14th century, has a north doorway, possibly Norman: the oak seats, curiously carved with shields and initial letters, were restored in 1857: in the south transept is a slab, supposed to mark the burial place of the founder, and here also is an altar-tomb with the incised effigy of a priest, vested, and holding a chalice, and on the sides figures of St. Catherine and St. Mary Magdalene, and three shields of arms, showing the alliances of the Tracy family; the upper slab also bears, in Norman-French, an invocatory inscription for Sir William Tracy, rector of this parish, ob. 1321, who founded a chantry in the church, and dedicated it to these saints;

The bell ringers of Mortehoe in 1926. Left to right: Geo. Smaldon (church warden), Revd T. Daffen, Messrs Alf Smith, E. Norman, T. Watts, W. Hill and A. Brown.

Fore Street, showing the Kings Arms Hotel on the left.

Extracts from Kelly: 'Northam is a parish and village standing on an eminence commanding a beautiful view of Barnstaple and Bideford Bay, and of Lundy Island... The parish is governed by an Urban District Council of twelve members, constituted under ... the "Local Government Act 1894" .... The living is a vicarage, with the chapelry of Westward Ho! annexed ... there are Congregational and Wesleyan chapels at Northam, and a Wesleyan Chapel at Northam Ridge (N.B. the former Landcross chapel). The Pebble, or "Boulder Ridge" at the mouth of the Taw and Torridge ... is a great natural curiosity ... this remarkable barrier extends about 2 miles in a straight line, like an artificial embankment, it is about 50 ft wide and 20 ft high and consists of rolled slate-stone, or pebbles, which vary in size from half a foot to 2 feet in diameter; it is singularly uniform and compact, on the one side sloping steeply to the turf of the Burrows; on the other, at a less inclination, to a broad area of sand, but scarcely a pebble is to be found on the turf or the shore beyond the base of the ridge. The shore scene is exceedingly wild ... at low water the dangerous bar is seen stretching athwart the entrance of the rivers; ... on the sea coast is a remarkable and interesting common called "The Burrows" fenced on two sides for the space of 3 miles by a vast barrier of boulders, surrounded and smoothed by the waves and described in the Rev. Charles Kingsley's *Westward Ho!*. A revel is held yearly on Whit Monday. The neighbourhood abounds in antiquities. At Kenwith Castle are the remains of fortifications, in the attack on which, in AD 877–8 the Danes, under Hubba, were defeated by the Saxons, under Alfred, and their Raven standard captured, a spot, still known as "Bloody Corner" is traditionally regarded as the scene of a duel between two of the chieftains.'

Children in the Square, *c.* 1874.

A street view.

One of Northam's vicars, with a group of ladies outside the Lifeboat Shed.

Folland's house.

This may be a view of North Street from the Square.

A parade through Fore Street. Devon Yeomanry were camped at Northam Burrows in February and March 1897.

Playing on the beach, *c.* 1911.

WESTWARD HO! a charming watering place, in the parish of Northam, has been so called from the Rev. Chas. Kingsley's novel of that name, the scene of which is chiefly laid in this vicinity; it is situated on the Northam Burrows, an extensive common of about 1,000 acres, stretching westward towards the shore of Bideford bay, on the coast of the bay between Baggy and Hartland points, into which flow the rivers Taw and Torridge, and is 2½ miles north-west from Bideford station on the London and South Western railway, 222½ from London by the London and South Western railway, via Bideford, and 242½ by the Great Western railway, with a station on the Bideford, Westward Ho! and Appledore railway, and is in the North Western division of the county and petty sessional division of Bideford. The inhabitants of Northam have from time immemorial had a right of pasturage on this large common, and it is greatly to be regretted that no sufficient measures are taken to restrain the encroachments of the tidal waters, which much diminish both its value and extent. Zoophytes of all kinds are to be found in abundance among the rocks, and the locality generally is rich in objects of interest to the antiquarian and geologist; a singular and very beautiful pebble ridge bounds a wide beach of sand on the one side and the extensive common on the other. There is a large and well-appointed hotel, with an excellent billiard room and good facilities for golf playing, besides many excellent lodging houses, bathing establishments, with spacious swimming baths, and good private residences; its picturesque situation and many natural beauties combine to make this one of the most attractive and popular of English watering places. The climate is equal, if not superior, to any in England, being mild but bracing, and the winter is on a par with that of the Riviera. The church of the Holy Trinity, erected in 1870 as a chapel of ease to Northam, is an edifice of stone, in the Early English style, from designs by Mr. Oliver, architect, of Barnstaple, consisting of chancel, nave, aisles, south porch and a western turret containing 2 bells: there are 400 sittings: divine service is conducted by the clergy of Northam. Here is also a Baptist chapel. Here is the Royal North Devon Golf Club and there is also a Union club. The Great Nassau Baths, the property of Mr. George J. Taylor, are 150 feet long, 55 wide and from 8 to 4 deep. Here is also a coastguard station. The United Services College was established in 1874, in order to supply to sons of officers in the two services a public school education of the highest class at a moderate cost: the school is conducted on the model of the great public schools and in conformity with the principles of the Church of England: the course of instruction is such as to qualify for the Universities and professions as well as to prepare for the Services: boys are admitted from 8 to 15 years of age and remain until 18: there is a junior school a short distance from the upper school, for boys between 8 and 12: substantial exhibitions are maintained for sons of officers of the Navy and Army and of all Government services: Rev. Francis William Tracy M.A. head master. G. J. Taylor esq. of Abbotsham Court, is the chief landowner.

Post, M. O. & T. O., T. M. O., S. B., Express Delivery, Parcel & Annuity & Insurance Office.—Miss E. E. Keyte, sub-postmistress. Letters through Bideford, delivery commences at 8.5 a.m. & 12.40 noon & 5 p.m.; dispatched at 9.10 a.m. & 2.10 & 6 p.m.; no delivery or dispatch on sundays

Wall Letter Box, Buckleigh, cleared at 7.30 a.m. & 12.20 & 5.25 p.m. & The Grove, cleared at 7.40 a.m. & 12.30 & 5.40 p.m. week days only

Chief of Coastguard, John Fogwill

Messrs. Dymond, Son & Blackmore's omnibuses & brakes run to & from Bideford frequently throughout the day

A general view.

Westward Ho! Pier. The Northam Burrows Promenade and Landing Pier Co. was floated in the summer of 1864 – it was intended to be profit-making. The pier was to project 600 ft from the shore at the little promontory by the side of seafield and to have a pier head with a space for refreshment rooms and a bandstand. The pier was built with much difficulty, and it collapsed twice during its construction due to wind and wave damage. It was finally finished and opened to the public on 10 July 1875. It was demolished by its builders ten years later.

Early sea-bathers at Westward Ho!

Westward Ho! from the Appledore Road.

Bathing tents by the Pebble Ridge. Dressing and undressing on the popular parts of the beach was prohibited, and people often had to ask permission to pay to put up a tent for a few hours, as parts of the beach were privately owned.

The view from above of the United Services College.

Opening the new sea wall in 1928.

The pebble ridge, *c.* 1900.

The pebble ridge and slipway, *c.* 1950s.

Possibly the Golden Bay Hotel.

The dreaded fourth bunker!

Members of the Royal North Devon Golf Club, founded in 1863.

Upper Lodge, Westward Ho!, c. 1925.

The old forge below Kipling Tors.

WESTLEIGH (or Leigh West) is a parish and village, near the river Torridge, 2 miles north-east from Bideford station on the Torrington branch of the London and South Western railway and 7 south-west from Barnstaple, in the North Western division of the county, Fremington hundred, Barnstaple union, Bideford petty sessional division and county court district, rural deanery of Barnstaple and archdeaconry and diocese of Exeter. The church of St. Peter is an ancient building of stone, in the Early English style, consisting of chancel, nave, aisles, transept, south porch and an embattled western tower containing 6 bells, recast by Taylor and Co. of Loughborough, in 1881: there are memorial windows to Thomas Berry esq. of Eastleigh, d. 1802; the Rev. John Torr M.A. 34 years vicar, d. 1835, and Jane, his wife, d. 1885; Gen. Thomas and Archibald Cleveland esq. cornet, 17th Lancers, who fell at Inkerman, 5th November, 1854; and to whom there is also a monument in the church: the west window is a memorial to Robert Pickard R.N. d. 17 March, 1894: the church was restored in 1880-82, at a cost of £1,292, under the direction of Mr. J. F. Gould, architect, of Barnstaple, and now affords 320 sittings.

EASTLEIGH, 1 mile east, on the road from Bideford to Barnstaple, and SOUTHCOTT, half a mile south, are hamlets. Southcott Barton is a very interesting old house in the Elizabethan style, the ceilings in some of the rooms display fine stucco work, and there is an old oak staircase and front door: it is now occupied as a farmhouse by Mr. Richard Balsdon.

Post Office.—William John Lemon, sub-postmaster. Letters through Bideford arrive at 8.45 a.m. & 6 p.m.; letter box cleared for mails at 8.40 a.m. & 5.55 p.m. No arrival or dispatch on sundays. Postal orders are issued here, but not paid. The nearest money order & telegraph office is at Instow, 2 miles distant

Wall Letter Box, Eastleigh, cleared at 8.10 a.m. & 6.10 p.m week days only

A School Board of 5 members was formed October 10th, 1872; Frederick Lee, Eastleigh, clerk to the board

Board School (mixed), built in 1876, at a cost of £860, for 90 children; average attendance, 60; Miss E. M. Rea, mistress

A view of the village.

Croyde Bay.

WOOLACOMBE BAY, about 1 mile south, and now a favourite seaside resort, is famous for its firm and broad sands, which extend about 3 miles along the shore. The fine hotel here was enlarged in 1897 so as to afford accommodation for over 150 visitors. It stands in its own pleasure grounds of 5 acres, adjoining golf links, and commands a pleasant view seaward. Several villa residences and lodging houses have also been built. Here is a chapel of ease to the parish church, with 220 sittings, and a Bible Christian chapel. The Working Men's club has the use of the Parish room from October to April, which contains reading, smoking and billiard rooms. The Royal Meteorological Society maintains a station here of the second order; observations are regularly made by E. Henshall esq. C.E., F.R.M.S.

Post, M. O. & T. O., T. M. O., S. B., Express Delivery, Parcel & Annuity & Insurance Office (Railway Sub-office. Letters should have R.S.O. North Devon added).—George Conibear, sub-postmaster. Letters received at 6.25 a.m. & 4.30 p.m.; dispatched (June to Oct.) 9.30 a.m. 1 & 7.10 p.m.; sunday, arrive 6.25 a.m.; dispatched 7.10 p.m

Post, M. O. & T. O., T. M. O., S. B., Express Delivery, Parcel & Annuity & Insurance Office, Woolacombe.—Francis Beer, sub-postmaster. Letters received through Mortehoe R.S.O. North Devon, arrive 7.35 a.m. 4.15 & 5.30 p.m.; dispatched at 9.30 (June to Oct.), 12.15 & 6.25 p.m.; sunday, 9.35 a.m

Wall Letter Boxes.—Mortehoe hotel, cleared on week days at 12.25 & 6.35 p.m.; sunday, 9.45 a.m. Railway station, cleared on week days at 9.45 a.m. & 4 p.m. & the Grange, cleared on week days at 12.50 & 6.30 p.m

A School Board of 5 members was formed Feb. 17, 1875; Wm. Henry Huxtable, 2 Clock Tower buildings, High street, Ilfracombe, clerk to the board; James Conibear, attendance officer

Board School (mixed), built in 1887, for 98 children; average attendance, 50; Charles Scanes, master

Railway Station, James Bertie Lodder, station master; cabs to meet all trains

A view of the village towards Morte Point.

The old Lifeboat House.

Woolacombe Bay Hotel; Mr D.A. Lockwood was the Manager; Kelly states 'this splendid hotel commands a most delightful sea view, and is situated in its own extensive pleasure grounds which slope down to the far famed Woolacombe Sands; golf links adjoining grounds; conveyances meet all trains to and from Mortehoe Station'.

Another view of the Woolacombe Bay Hotel

The first house to be built on the sea front, date unknown.

Barricane Beach, showing Bennett & Parker tea tents, pre-1914. The beach was famous for its shells.

Above Barricane Beach on the old Woolacombe to Mortehoe Road.

Barricane Beach, pre-1914.

Bathing machines on Woolacombe beach, pre-1914.

Landkey children going for an outing in a steam lorry.

I have included these last few photographs from our Archive to show that our grandparents and great-grandparents enjoyed their summer outings just as much as we do today. I wonder whether they would have envied us, or been outraged by all our freedom of dress and behaviour.

Paddling at Woolacombe, 8 August 1923 – possibly Daisy Blackmore and her father.

The Curtis family from Beaford on a picnic at Westward Ho!, c. 1910.

Paddling at Ilfracombe, 1911.

An outing from Chulmleigh.

Catching the paddle-steamer, 11 September 1914.

The Revd and Mrs Barnard of Roborough with their family; he was blind.

This photograph is jokingly entitled 'The flight into Egypt'; Clovelly donkey and riders, September 1914.

Archie Cole's bus, climbing Porlock Hill with an outing from Landkey.

The optimists!

The Quay at Appledore, *c.* 1935.

RECORD OFFICES

The Devon County Record Office and West Country Studies Library, Exeter, Devon.
The North Devon Record Office and the Atheneum Library, Barnstaple, N. Devon.

ACKNOWLEDGEMENTS

Mrs Joy Slocombe, of the Ilfracombe Museum for loaning photographs and providing information. Mr J. Rowe and Mrs Marjorie Snetzler of the North Devon Atheneum for allowing me access to the Atheneum Library and to Marjorie in particular for all her help with information. All the members of the public who, over the years, have donated their photographs and recalled their family histories to add to the Archive. The staff of the Beaford Centre who have had to persuade the public that the Archive was closed temporarily to allow me peace and quiet for 'the Books'. Michael Gullick and Rodney Cooper, two of our Employment Trainees who have done a great deal of the photographic printing for me. And, finally, my colleague and friend, Janet Williamson, who has assisted me with the compilations all the way through, sorting through captions, putting photocopies ready for paste-up and turning my incredibly illegible scribbles into neat typescript!

BIBLIOGRAPHY

Kelly's Directory of Devon, 1902.
Postcard views of N. Devon, Tom Bartlett, 1987.
Views of Old Devon, Tom Bartlett.
Views of Old Devon, Rosemary A. Lauder, 1982.
Bideford in old picture postcards, Muriel Goaman, 1982.
Bideford Gazette, Silver Jubilee Supplement, May 1935.
Various copies of the *North Devon Journal*.
Aspects of Devon History, R.R. Selman, 1985.
The Local Historian's Encyclopaedia, John Richardson, 1986.
Strong's Industries of N. Devon, David & Charles, reprint, 1971.